SONGS OF JOY

On our lips
there were
songs of joy.

SONGS OF JOY

New Meditations on the Psalms for Every Day of the Year

JOAN D. CHITTISTER, OSB

A Crossroad Book
The Crossroad Publishing Company
New York

This printing: 1999

The Crossroad Publishing Company
370 Lexington Avenue, New York, NY 10017

Copyright © 1997 by Joan D. Chittister, OSB

Printed in the United States of America

Library of Congress Cataloging-in-Publication Data

Chittister, Joan.
    Songs of joy : new meditations on the Psalms for every day of the
year / [Joan Chittister].
        p.   cm.
    ISBN 0-8245-1661-3 (pbk.)
    1. Bible. O.T. Psalms – Meditations. 2. Devotional calendars.
3. Spiritual life – Christianity – Meditations.   I. Title.
BS1430.4C49   1997
242'.2–dc21   97-1676
                                                               CIP

ACKNOWLEDGMENTS

The production of personal reflections may seem at first to be a very simple process. As a matter of fact, it takes time, a lot of it, and resources, a wide variety of them. In this case, the reflection comes out of a lifetime of saying the psalms and trying to build a bridge in my own heart between what scripture holds as eternal truths in one era and the search for truths in our own lives in this one. The process engages me yet. In what way, I ask myself, do the learnings and insights and revelations of one generation guide another? In what way do our cosmic lives intersect over ages and issues? Is life always unique or unique only in that each of us lives out every universal topic differently? Clearly, it takes a lifetime to pursue those questions actively.

It also takes resources to search for insights through time and then make them available for our time. The reflections, with all their limitations, I myself take responsibility for attempting. The resources, however, have come from the people around me whose own gifts have made this endeavor possible. I am daily grateful.

Mary Lou Kownacki, OSB, is the muse who whispers in my ear in an irritatingly unarguable fashion. She envisioned this work and prodded me unmercifully until I finished it.

Anne McCarthy, OSB, provides the editorial direction and evaluation that gives the surety that what is said is said with accuracy and quality.

Susan Doubet, OSB, gives hours to the preparation of the materials I need to complete it, the sources I use to support it, and the contacts it takes to maintain it with a personal touch.

Susan Freitag, OSB, shepherds every mailing through with precision and care, month after month after month.

Judith Allison does with careful and competent graphic design what I try to do with words — bring beauty, bring strength, bring clarity.

To all of these women, whose gifts make the Monastic Way, these Songs of Joy, possible, I am forever indebted. The observations may be mine but it is their gifts, their generosity that make this book possible.

INTRODUCTION

The psalms are the oldest prayers in the Judeo-Christian tradition. There are 150 of them and, like hymns to-day, they were written for multiple occasions. They are a lexicon of the human condition. They trace the human condition back thousands of years. They assure us that our own hopes and fears, desires and emotions are just like those of the rest of humankind. Say each month's verse from the psalms before every reading. By the end of the month, say it from memory. It will find a soft spot in your heart. Most of all, it will bring your heart the comfort of the ages.

JANUARY

PSALM 90

All our days
pass away;
our life is over
in a breath.
Seventy is the sum
of our years
or eighty
if we are strong.

Time is one of the few dimensions of life that has no properties. It is not short or tall, heavy or thin, old or young. It just is. Time has only those qualities that we ourselves give to it. We are spiritual people with very material things to do. That's how we know that one is the other. The spiritual life is the way we live the material one — the attitudes we bring to it, the purposes we pursue in it, the work we put into it, the sense of the transcendent that we develop in it. Time is sacred. Time is holy. Time is the raw material of the sacramental. Somehow or other we have to understand that this life is our life and the way we spend it is the kind of person we will, in the end, come to be.

January 1: Time is one of the greatest problems we have in life. We complain regularly that we either have too little of it — or we have too much of it. That can only mean one thing: we're not doing what we want to be doing at any given moment. Time isn't the problem. It's all the things that crowd or block the way we want to spend it. Look at those things. They'll tell you plenty about your life, your values, and your future.

January 2: The psalmist reminds us that however long life is, it's still far too short to waste. But what precisely does it mean to "waste" time? The Puritans would say that we are wasting time when we are not engaged in some kind of useful work. Americans would say that it's a period when we're not moving toward a given goal. The hedonist would say that it's when we're not enjoying ourselves. The psalmist would say that it's a period in which we fail to live life fully, to be aware of it and its meaning for us at a given moment. Which one are you living? Is it good for you?

January 3: It's fear of time that causes us to age prematurely. Life is not the process of getting older; it is the process of getting better.

January 4: Rabindranath Tagore writes, "The butterfly counts not months but moments, and has time enough." One of the major mistakes of life may be to put everything off until a later period. It's the "as soon as" syndrome. "I'll go back to school, I'll take some time for myself, I'll visit them, I'll take guitar lessons as soon as..." everything else is finished. But the other things are never finished. When there is no time in life for good things now, life is hopelessly skewed.

January 5: To waste the present regretting the past makes life a sickly place. It's what you're doing now that counts. If you owe the past a debt, pay it; don't wallow in it and waste the beauty of this moment too. If someone still owes you a debt, forget it. They're not ready yet.

January 6: "Procrastination," Don Marquis wrote, "is the art of keeping up with yesterday." The things we put off doing — the calls we don't make, the letters we don't write, the jobs we don't do until the last moment — haunt us until we do. That haunting takes the joy out of everything else.

January 7: A year is nothing but the amount of time it takes for the earth to go completely around the sun before it begins the trip all over again. The completion of a year, then, is not a sign that things are ending. It is surely much more the realization that life repeats itself unendingly. We have a chance to do everything again, better this time, more comfortably this time, more joyfully this time.

January 8: There is no use waiting for something new to happen. We have to make it happen. If you don't like your life, change it. If you can't change it, you can enlarge it so that what you don't like is only part of your life — not all of it.

January 9: Time is an almost invariable measure of the quality of life. When time and schedules control us more than we control them, our life is out of control. Then it's time to take stock and take charge again.

January 10: Sometimes we escape the things we fear in life by scheduling ourselves too tightly to think. Make a time study this week. Put down everything you did. Which of the things you agreed to do did you really want to do? Which ones did you take despite the fact that you didn't want to do them? Why did you do what you didn't want to do? That's your problem, not your schedule's. Face it.

January 11: The older we get, the shorter life gets. Then we understand that life is too short for fighting, too short for pleasing, too short to waste on things that do not leave the world better than when we came into it.

January 12: Do at least one thing you really like every single day. Do you like to be alone? Say so and do it. Do you like to read or play the piano or paint? Say so and do it. Do you like to spend time with friends? Call them up. Plan it. Don't simply let life go by. You'll regret it if you do.

January 13: Frankly, I think that New Year's resolutions are fruitless, irritating, silly. It's the resolution I make every day that counts. Make one every morning and every night. You will feel terrific.

January 14: Time is what God gives us so that we can grow into life slowly, come to understand it, savor it. Wisdom is simply the consciousness of how foolish we've been in the past. That's why it usually comes with age. Once we've done all those things, we realize how foolish, how dangerous, how essentially shallow they were.

January 15: Every period of life has its own task and its own meaning. There is no time that is useless.

What was the task of your last stage of life? What do you think is the task of this one? Talk to someone about both of them. Draw from their wisdom as well as your own.

January 16: Sometimes I think that the period in life in which we begin to lose our memories may be the only time in every person's history when we really concentrate on the present. It is a grace, in other words, given to those who raced through every other period without noticing.

January 17: Time is meant to free us for life but instead time enslaves us. Instead of listening to the people we're with, we keep checking our watches to make sure that we're on time for the person who's coming next. We live with our minds on something else instead of the presence of God in the present. So we miss our children growing up. We miss the middle years of marriage. We miss the calls within us to live life in new ways. We lose time and think we're living. How sad. Be here — now.

January 18: Time tempers us and gives a reason to live. We are not simply souls in orbit. We are people in relationship to the rest of the world. We are here for a purpose. There are great human questions emerging at this crossover point in history. What is your position on them? How did you arrive at it? Are you doing anything to help resolve the situation?

January 19: Don't confuse balance with arithmetic. A life divided into multiple segments of a twenty-four-hour day is not necessarily "balanced." It is only scheduled. That life is balanced that has meaningful pieces of life regularly recognized: family, solitude, spirituality, work, others, leisure, play. Which one of those is consuming the other dimensions in your life? List them in their order of time consumption. Which dimension of life should you be increasing? Time is short.

January 20: "Today is, tomorrow is not," the Hindustani proverb says. There's something you're putting off. Don't wait any longer.

January 21: "Everything must wait its turn...peach blossoms for the second month and chrysanthemums for the ninth," say the Japanese. Part of living well is learning to wait. Some things can't be rushed, only nurtured.

January 22: Time is a ruthless teacher. What we do not learn in this period of life awaits us in the next. The young learn to listen and to work, the middle-aged to risk and to build, the retired to let go and begin again, and the elderly to be alone and to wait. Each of them is a dimension of the God-life. Each of them teaches us to become more like God. Consider them carefully. Which of them needs the most attention from you right now?

January 23: We must spend life in ways that bring us to growth. We must, then, spend life on ourselves, of course. People who pay no attention to their own needs go through life resentful or underdeveloped. But we must not spend life only on ourselves; though the self teaches us much, it does not teach us all. It teaches us only what we need to know. And what we need to know, we must learn someplace else.

January 24: It is a paltry life indeed that centers only on itself. Think for a moment how you have spent your time. If you died tomorrow, who besides yourself would notice? Whose life besides your own would lose something? If you can't name two hands' worth of people, maybe you ought to give some thought to joining a service organization and volunteering your time.

January 25: We are the only hands God has. Creation goes on creating through us. What are you doing for the world at this time in your life that God wants done? That's why you were put here, after all.

January 26: "It is not enough to be busy," Thoreau wrote. So are ants. "What is important is what we are busy about." There is a difference between the restful and the frivolous; the enjoyable and the disgusting; the playful and the destructive. It's what I do with my time that counts. The question is, Is my major concern worth a life?

January 27: "I would rather lose in a cause that must someday prevail," Wilkie said, "than triumph in a cause that must someday fail." Don't be discouraged if what you have spent your life to achieve has yet to be accomplished. Millions of people knew that slavery was wrong a long time before it ended. Millions of people knew that colonialism was wrong a long time before it collapsed. Millions of people knew that the treatment of women like adult children was wrong a long time before they were allowed to go to school. History is a record of great ideas defeated in their earliest stages. But truth will win out in the long run. What matters now is simply that you and I do what we can in our own lifetime to hasten the process. Spend your time on the big things.

January 28: Complete this sentence: In every life there should be...Do you have it? What is it that you want most in life right now and have least time for? What are you choosing instead? Why? Look at that very closely. It's telling you something you need to attend to.

January 29: It's not easy; in fact, it's often impossible simply to block out situations that are less than what we want, less than what we need in life. One set of obligations cancels the other set of needs. I need to work my way through school so I can't study as much as I would like. I need to raise the children so I can't leave a loveless marriage. I need to support a family so I can't leave this job. I need to finish this project so I can't leave this group. What then? Then we must find that spot in ourselves that still knows life and cultivate it. Then we need to draw life from borrowed joy. Don't stay in the rut, in other words; find the thing that stirs your heart and make room for it before your heart turns to stone and there is no room left for anything. That alone will take courage enough.

January 30: Indifference, apathy, distance are the curses of life. They leave us with a schedule and no soul. Do something purposeful in life — set a goal and achieve it — even if it is nothing more than changing the furniture around in the room. Don't just go through life like tumbleweed in the wind.

January 31: Filling time is not always the way to use time best. Sometimes we learn a great deal more by just sitting and thinking about it, looking at it and taking stock of it, comparing our lives with the lives of those around us. This life is the only one we have. What a pity to come to the end of it saying, "I could have ... I should have ... but I didn't."

FEBRUARY

PSALM 126

When God brought Israel
back to Zion,
it seemed like a dream.
Then our mouths were
filled with laughter;
on our lips there were
songs of joy.

This month's psalm talks to us about laughing, a too-often overlooked spiritual discipline. The important thing to realize about this psalm is that it takes place after the destruction of Jerusalem and the Babylonian captivity. These people had suffered mightily. But in their freedom they did not become bitter. They learned to laugh — and so must we.

The function of humor is not to make light of serious things. The function of a good story is to enable us to see life differently than we ordinarily do, to topple the mighty from their thrones so that all of us become equal again.

Humor gives spirit to a people when they have no other defense. Jews delighted, for instance, in telling the story of the old man in top hat and phylacteries who appeared at the local Gestapo station. He was holding an ad in his hand that called for young, healthy Aryans to promise service for the Führer. "What are you doing here?" the commandant asked the old Jew. "I'm answering this ad," the old man said. "What?" the commandant asked incredulously. "That's ridiculous. You're not young." "No," the old man said, "I'm seventy-three." "And you're certainly not Aryan." "No," the old man said, "I'm Jewish — both sides." "And you're obviously not committed to serving the Führer." "No," the old man said, "I wouldn't do a single thing for that man." "Then why are you here?" the com-

mandant insisted angrily." "Vell," the old Jew said, "I just come down to tell you that on me you shouldn't count."

Point: Humor gives a people dignity in situations that denigrate them. Laughter gives us relief from the burden of dailiness. No amount of coercion can break an unbreakable spirit, humor teaches us. And someday that cagey old man, buried deep in our spirits, becomes the patron saint of our own silent, laughing resistance to systems that reject us but cannot survive our disdain. Humor cuts oppressors down to size, takes their sting away, renders them powerless to destroy us. Don't give in to what diminishes you. Learn to laugh at it and reduce its power over you.

February 1: We've been misled. Nineteenth-century spirituality became, like the rest of society, very mechanistic. We got the impression that if we did certain exercises, said certain prayers, kept certain rules the process would produce a kind of assembly-line holiness. It was all very serious, very acidic, very rigorous stuff. What a silly thought. Every child knows that if getting to heaven is that dour, it can't be worth it.

February 2: My God is a God who laughs. And why not? Here we are — racing through life assuming that everything depends on us. And nothing is perfect yet. Wouldn't you think we would get used to imperfection? No wonder God finds us so funny. Well, better that than unbearable.

February 3: Here's a good idea: the next time you're really upset about the important things in life — like being late for an appointment, or watching your dog knock over your best vase, or finding out that the car won't start, or discovering that the screwdriver isn't where it's supposed to be — laugh. The problem will disappear because nothing is a "problem" unless we call it that.

February 4: Laughter reduces tension, halts judgment, stops the inner turmoil that comes from being too serious about too little. Death is serious. Loss is serious. A change of schedule is not serious. Irritating, maybe. Exasperating, maybe. But not serious. Laugh.

February 5: Never confuse humor and ridicule. Humor cleanses the soul of tension; ridicule creates tension. It makes a person the butt of public derision and takes joy out of life. It hurts. When we laugh at what is not a mere lapse of the normal, not changeable, not the triumph of innocence over pomp, that is not humor. To laugh at physical defects, at ethnic characteristics, at human effort is not funny. That is laughter become a weapon.

February 6: Laughter is a sign of mental health, balance, perspective, maturity. It is also a sign of holiness — for all the same reasons. Don't separate the two — it makes holiness a mental illness.

February 7: The Koran says, "They deserve paradise who make their companions laugh." Salvation is in our hands. All we have to do is to stop complaining. And giggle a little.

February 8: To laugh at those who have no power over us — to laugh at children and minorities and women — is to become the oppressor. It wields derision over the head of the powerless like an axe. How sad. How sinful.

February 9: "Of all days," De Chamfort wrote in 1796, "the day on which one has not laughed is the one most surely wasted." Oh, no, we say. A wasted day is a day in which we don't get finished all the work we intend to finish when we get up in the morning. But the work is never done. So, if we live life by those standards, every day of life is a waste. My suggestion: Forget the work. Change your standards of success and laugh. Not only is it easier, it may leave the world a great deal better off than one more ream of paper printed to fill a wastebasket, one more room cleaned, one more routine hoop jumped.

February 10: The thing about laughter is you have to take it seriously. That, or end up a shriveled-up excuse for half a person.

February 11: February: The bills come in, the winds get chill, the days stay short, Lent appears on a cold horizon. We've never needed laughter more. So make some for somebody and you'll feel better yourself. It's called the recognition of grace. And, yes, when you quit spending energy being depressed about everything else, there's plenty of it around.

February 12: "Tomorrow, do thy worst," John Dryden wrote, "for I have lived today." Think of it: What worse can happen that you haven't already survived? So take the bad and make it as good as you can. The Irish have it right. After all, what else do you think an Irish wake is all about?

February 13: Laughter is holy. Why? Because it turns the obstacles in life into the play of the angels.

February 14: When children pour milk over their heads, they laugh. It is a lesson we forget far too young in life. All of life was made for enjoying. Little has the power to destroy us unless we give ourselves over to it.

February 15: Try going through today laughing at what you would ordinarily growl, complain, or snap at. Then, tonight ask yourself what happened to you as a result. The fact is that we have the power within us to make ourselves happy or unhappy. Complaining makes us miserable. Laughing gives us perspective, serenity, and calm. Try it. Just one day. I dare you to be happy.

February 16: "Among those whom I like or admire, I can find no common denominator, but among those whom I love, I can: all of them make me laugh,"

W. H. Auden wrote. If you find yourself running out of friends, it might be worth a try.

February 17: Unfortunately, it often takes great tragedy to discover that we have allowed ourselves to take other things far too seriously. Try to cultivate the relaxed grasp before things you should have put down voluntarily are taken away from you without your permission.

February 18: The spirituality of humor lies in using humor to amuse but not to hurt, to uplift but not to denigrate, to lighten the environment but never to ridicule a person. There is no kindness like humor, no blessing like a smile when there's little or nothing to smile about.

February 19: We teach children the alphabet; we teach adults to drive; we teach students to count; we teach families to save money. We teach people all sorts of things that are functional. But we pay very little attention to what makes us human — like joy and care and balance. We want people to do and do and do, more and more and more. Maybe it's time we added humor to the human curriculum so that we could learn what life eventually teaches us all: that there is very little in life that is more important than life itself. And very little in life that deserves the degree of consternation we give it.

February 20: "If you're not allowed to laugh in heaven," Martin Luther wrote, "I don't want to go there." We should have known right off that the man was a saint.

February 21: "In this world there are only two tragedies," Oscar Wilde wrote. "One is not getting what you want; the other is getting it." Isn't it the truth? Learn to laugh. It's a survival mechanism.

February 22: We develop workshops on anger, we form support groups for family problems, we give courses in communication skills. Why do we treat as incidental the one thing that eases tension, reduces stress, and bonds strangers — humor, laughter, and human playfulness? Maybe it's because religion stressed the serious side of God without stressing at the same time the God who sends angels to save us from harm, who blows down walls with small horns, and who gives parties for five thousand with five fish. I'll take that God any day.

February 23: What did you laugh at today? What didn't you laugh at today that you should have, both for your sake and for everybody else's? What do both situations tell you about yourself?

February 24: Laughter is a very serious thing. It heals us physically, calms us emotionally, stabilizes us psychologically, and braces us spiritually. Laughter teaches us that the world does not end when plans go awry. It just goes on differently.

February 25: God save us from perfect people. They are such bores.

February 26: Happiness doesn't depend on what we have. Happiness depends on what we think. What are you unhappy about? Try changing your mind about it. Psychologists call the process of seeing circumstances from more than one perspective "reframing" a situation. Frankly, I think it's the spiritual ability to see the whole picture instead of only one part of it. It's an excursion into trust.

February 27: "My doctor gave me six months to live, but when I couldn't pay the bill he gave me six months more," Walter Matthau said. See what I mean? Just thinking the unthinkable makes us feel better in a minute.

February 28: "A cynic is not merely one who reads bitter lessons from the past; he is one who is prematurely disappointed in the future," Sydney Harris wrote. It's so easy to get into that rut. Only laughter fuels hope.

February 29: T. S. Eliot wrote: "The years between fifty and seventy are the hardest. You are always being asked to do things you are not decrepit enough yet to turn down." (But when you consider the alternative...)

February 30 (if there were a February 30): "Those who laugh, last." Remember, you heard it here, second!

MARCH

PSALM 73

What else have I
in heaven but you?
Apart from you
I want nothing on earth.
My heart leaps for joy,
for you, O God,
are my portion forever.

*I*t's not easy to write about simplicity in a complex world. It is even harder to think about it. The concept seems to evoke one of two reactions: guilt — "I know I have too much, but I don't have a clue how else to live" — or ridicule — "I know I can't have everything. Wherever would I put it?" The fact is that frugality is cheap simplicity. Simplicity requires a great deal more from us than simply getting rid of the gadgets we don't want or the surplus we don't need. Simplicity requires that we learn how to live a centered life, to "make God our portion," in a world that tears our days, our lives, our psyches into tangled shreds.*

March 1: "It is not easy to find happiness in ourselves and impossible to find it elsewhere," Agnes Repplier wrote. There may be no better explanation of "simplicity" anywhere. It strips life down to its lowest common denominator: the simple joy of life itself.

March 2: It's when we set out to shape every element of life to our own designs that we lose all sense of simplicity. "Going with the flow" is a very liberating spiritual discipline that is good for interpersonal relationships, social life, and ulcers.

March 3: "You, O God, are my portion forever," the psalmist says. Since inheritance and ownership of land were such important elements of family life in the Middle East, to say that God was all you really wanted in life, the "portion" of life you were really seeking, the "riches" you counted on, was a major spiritual statement. In fact, do you know anyone who can say it now? Can you say it yourself?

March 4: "All I want is a little more than I'll ever get," Ashleigh Brilliant wrote. What a sad commentary on the unsatisfied life. Settle down. Take care of what's missing inside and you will never notice what's missing outside.

March 5: Pretending to be something we are not—a little bit better placed, a touch more educated than we really are, a family of more means than we actually have — puts us in a position of eternal jeopardy. Someone will surely find out. Wouldn't it be less tension-producing, let alone a demonstration of holy simplicity, just to be honest about it all?

March 6: The hard truth may be that simplicity of life is not necessarily life without things. In fact, life without necessities — grueling, unfair, and involuntary poverty — is not simplicity at all. No, simplicity may far more properly be life without clutter, life without compulsions, life without a need to control, life that is focused by single-hearted vision than it is something as easy as life without things.

March 7: Simplicity of life is what the poet-president Sister Madeleva Wolff, CSC, called "the habitually relaxed grasp." It isn't what we have accumulated, in other words, that measures the simplicity of our lives; it's what we're willing to let go of when we must, when we should.

March 8: When people with rigid dietary fancies put other people under a great deal of strain cooking for them, I can't help but wonder how really simple that is. When people handle their own schedules very well because they simply refuse to have their personal priorities interrupted by anybody else's needs, is that living "the simple life"? Everybody else is forced to bend to suit them — and so everybody else's lives wind up more and more intricate, involved, difficult as a result. So who is really practicing simplicity of life in these cases? Simplicity, I am convinced, is far more than having life on our own terms whatever its effect on others.

March 9: Simplicity of life in a complex and complicated world is marked, I think, by four characteristics: a life is simple if it is honest, if it is unencumbered, if it is open to the ideas of others, if it is serene in the midst of a mindless momentum that verges on the chaotic. And which of these do you do best? And which of these do you do poorly?

March 10: At base, simplicity of life has a great deal more to do with authenticity than it does with things — or else it would be a virtue only for those who had things to forego. Then simplicity would have more to do with classism, with a kind of social play called "voluntary simplicity," than with an attitude of mind that lets us stand in the midst of our worlds naked and unafraid, sure of soul and unencumbered by the seductiveness of the unnecessary and the cosmetic.

March 11: Isn't simplicity really what the ancients called "purity of heart," that single-minded search for the essence of life rather than a grasping after its frills, whatever shape those might take in our various worlds?

March 12: Here's a test: James Thurber wrote that people "Should strive to learn before they die / What they are running from, and to, and why." Simplicity, in other words, is knowing what my life is really all about. Which of Thurber's questions are you able to answer?

March 13: "Life is not meant to be easy, my child," George Bernard Shaw wrote, "but take courage; it can be delightful." Simplicity takes life as it comes, assumes the best of everyone, doesn't turn perfectly normal situations into instances of hysterical concern. Wednesdays have been following Tuesdays for eons now and, we may assume, will continue to do so for ages to come. Cool it. Most of what you are concerned about today, you won't remember tomorrow.

March 14: It is one thing to know who we are. It is another thing to be indifferent to the many phases of life's meandering ways. Today I have money and a job and a title. On some surprising day, I will not have even that. When that day comes, all the simplicity I have affected will be tested to the core. On that day, I will discover the hard truth that simplicity of life is life free of the things we own so that they do not own us.

March 15: To face society unfeigned and to walk through the world with hands and hearts unrestrained frees a person for the basics of life. Freedom is the real purpose, the real essence of simplicity.

March 16: We have insulated ourselves against life to such an extent that we can go for years without living it. Stereo systems vented from basement to bathroom make it impossible for us to ever appreciate silence. Television saves us from talking to the people we live with for years. Staying in touch with every dimension of life breeds the kind of simplicity that gives life texture, makes life true.

March 17: Simplicity is openness to the beauty of the present, whatever its shape, whatever its lack. Simplicity, clearly, leads to freedom of soul. When we cultivate a sense of "enoughness," when we learn to enjoy things for their own sakes, when we learn to be gentle even with what is lacking in ourselves, we find ourselves free to be where we are and to stop mourning where we are not. We find that simplicity is an antidote to depression.

March 18: The Desert Monastics tell this story: Abbot Mark once said to Abbot Arsenius, "It is good, is it not, to have nothing in our cell that just gives us pleasure? For example, I once knew a brother who had a little wildflower that came up in his cell and he pulled it out by the roots." "Well," said Abbot Arsenius, "that is all right. But each person should act according to her own spiritual way. And if one were not able to get along without the flower, she should plant it again." Simplicity is not the arithmetic of the soul. Simplicity of life is not really about things at all. Simplicity is about being able to take them — and to leave them.

March 19: The simple person pays close attention to the agitations that eat at the heart. It is our agitations that tell us where life has gone astray for us, has become unbearably complex and eternally confused. If we fret at every delay, become miserable at every change of plans, become miffed at every imagined slight, then God has been replaced in us by a god of our own making. Then the simple life, the sanctity of the present moment, disappears into oblivion. Then simplicity of heart becomes counterfeit.

March 20: No doubt about it: simplicity and serenity carry overtones of the same chord. Both of them ring of an imperturbability that comes from being rooted in a God who is Everything and who waits for us to find life at the center, beyond the clutter of the commonplace, beneath the delusion of the image, behind the things that become our gods — sterile, empty, smothering.

March 21: Simplicity and serenity, simplicity and honesty, simplicity and openness, simplicity and acceptance are synonyms too long kept secret. But without them simplicity itself is fraud.

March 22: "The closing years of life are like the end of a masquerade party, when the masks are dropped," Arthur Schopenhauer wrote. Only simplicity of life can prepare us for the moment. What masks are you wearing that need to be dropped if you are ever to really enjoy the liberation that comes with simplicity?

March 23: Etty Hillesum wrote from a German concentration camp, "My life is increasingly an inner one and the outer setting matters less and less." What is there in your outer life that tells you that you need to develop more of an inner one if the outer one is not to consume you?

March 24: Here's a thought: "To be without some of the things you want is an indispensable part of happiness," the philosopher Bertrand Russell said.

Simplicity simply demands that what we strive for we also have the internal fortitude to be able to live without.

March 25: "Live simply so that others may simply live," Mother Seton taught. Don't hoard. When you get something new, give the old one away to someone who needs it.

March 26: The number of things we own is not the total measure of simplicity, but acknowledging the amount of them is an exercise that prepares us to be simple under other circumstances. Think of three things you have that you could do without. Get rid of one of them this week. The pain you feel in doing so is the proof that you are still alive — and growing nicely.

March 27: Agitation and accumulation are signs of a lack of simplicity. Chop all the wood you want, give away all the clothes you own, romanticize the praises of the pioneer life, but simplicity has flown you by.

March 28: "What else have I in heaven but you?" the psalmist asks God. In the end, the simple life is all about having what we did or did not seek. Simplicity of life prepares us to see the Beyond before we are beyond it.

March 29: "My heart leaps for joy, for you, O God, are my portion forever." When we have God in life, we have it all. Then happiness comes. Not before. Not from anything else. Simplicity is the poetry of the soul.

March 30: "If we go down into ourselves we find that we possess exactly what we desire," Simone Weil wrote. Provided, of course, that we develop something there in the first place. Otherwise, we have to put our faith in things outside of us for happiness: things that come and go; things that promise what they cannot produce and that, when they go, leave us sad and bereft, empty and lost, full of nothing.

March 31: "There must be more to life than having everything," Maurice Sendak wrote. And there is, of course. It is simplicity, the capacity for not needing it in the first place.

APRIL

PSALM 51

You love
those who search
for truth.
In wisdom, center me,
for you know
my frailty.

The dictum "Know thyself," which appeared on the statue of the Oracle of Apollo at Delphi in sixth-century B.C. Greece, is one of the oldest directives in Western philosophy. It's good advice. We so often project onto other people the tendencies we fail to recognize in ourselves. In our time, however, the concern is as much about self-esteem as it is about self-knowledge. Both positions are valuable. But both of them are insufficient, I think.

Self-knowledge gives us perspective and self-esteem gives us confidence, but it's self-acceptance that gives us peace of heart. It implies, of course, that I know myself and value myself. Yet, unless I can simply start by accepting myself, it is possible that neither of the other two dimensions can ever come to life in me. Clearly, even if I know who I am, even if I admit the truth about myself, if I don't accept what I see there, I can never really value it. Worse, I'll live in fear that someone else will see to the core of me and reject me, too.

But, the psalmist teaches us, that's precisely where the God who birthed us, our loving Mother God, becomes the mainstay, not the menace of our lives. God knows exactly who we are. God knows our frailty. And God accepts it. And gathers it in. God loves us, not despite it, but because of it, because of the effort it implies and the trust it demands. There is glory in the clay of us. There is beauty in becoming. The static notion of life, the idea that we can become something and stay that way, is a false one. We face newness all our lives. We search all our days for truth. And God loves us for the seeking. What we need is not perfection. What we need is a center that stabilizes us in times of change, in us as well as around us.

April 1: "In wisdom, center me," the psalmist has us pray this month. Everybody is centered in something. In each of us there is that internal magnet that guides our decisions and occupies our thoughts. For some it's fear, for others it's ambition, for many it's social acceptance, for a portion of humanity it's independence, for real unfortunates it's perfection of one kind or another. When the internal lodestone is wisdom, however, we are able to take life as it is and just be happy that we learned from it instead of being crushed by it.

April 2: In this culture we put a lot of time on the presentation of the external self — the way we look, the way we talk, the kind of professional credentials we amass. We put very little time, on the other hand, on attending to the internal self — the way we think, the way we judge, the way we respond to the circumstances of life. But therein lies the real truth about ourselves. Follow those things and you will learn what you really need to know in life.

April 3: The nice thing about not being perfect is not being required to be. You can relax now. What's stopping you? That's what needs to be changed in you.

April 4: Think a minute: What are the two deepest desires of your soul for yourself? What's keeping you from attaining them?

April 5: "Life is full of internal dramas, instantaneous and sensational, played to an audience of one," Anthony Pail writes. Whatever you are struggling with internally right now is your call to the next stage of life. Treat it gently. Don't try either to stamp it out or to make it happen. Just ask yourself what you are being allowed to learn from it. That's wisdom.

April 6: If we were supposed to be perfect, we would have been made perfectible. As it is, we are a constantly evolving creature required only to be the best we can be in every circumstance. The trick lies in coming to recognize what the best really is in every situation. The growth lies in accepting ourselves even when, after sincerely trying, we miserably fail to do it. God will provide for the rest.

April 7: What is the purpose of self-hatred? All it does is make getting up in the morning harder and harder. Self-acceptance means that we can't wait for tomorrow in order to try again or try something new or just try for the sake of trying. Self-acceptance makes life one great, free, and wholehearted effort to live well.

April 8: We're such a goal-centered culture. We go on picnics and miss the scenery along the way; we work hard for promotions and miss the people we're working with now; we strive for the perfect life situation and lose the sense of what is good where we are. That's why we get fixated on "the good old days." What a shameful waste of life.

April 9: Anyone who says they want to be young again is either a fool or a liar. In the first place, the period of our youth was no easier than this one. Oftentimes harder, in fact. In the second place, the task of that time was to bring us to this one. There is something in the now for us that will make the future even better—if we can just keep moving toward it. Don't stop living just because life isn't perfect.

April 10: The world presents us with images which, if we can't meet them, lead to self-hatred. But one thing I know for sure: If women were really to be that thin and men were to be that skinny-hipped, there would be a lot more of those types on the street than there are. Work on the smile and you'll find that the figure won't count nearly as much.

April 11: "It is not the same to talk of bulls as it is to be in the bull ring," the Spanish say. Until you have gone through a thing yourself — through the death of a loved one, through the loss of a job, through a rejection — don't think you really understand it. Just listen to those who have, so that when you come to that moment yourself, you can take to it a store of wisdom that gives you trust in God's strange ways.

April 12: "The one who has mounted an elephant will not fear the bark of a dog," the Indian proverb teaches. Once we negotiate something difficult in life, everything lesser pales in its effect on us. That's why life is a process of going from strength to strength.

April 13: Life is something we learn about through its peak moments of deep pain and great joy. All the rest of the time we spend trying to assimilate both, to make sense of them, to make ourselves capable of both.

April 14: I write my life in my own blood. Anything else is sham. When I hurt, I'll know what hurt is all about. When I fail, I'll find out what survival is all about. When I love, I'll come to know what selflessness is all about. And when we know those things, we will be both wise and fully alive.

April 15: If I am sitting around saying, "I wish I were as smart as, as pretty as, as powerful as, as appreciated as..." someone else we know, we are light years away from self-acceptance.

April 16: Self-acceptance is not self-satisfaction. It is self-realization. It is the ability to see ourselves as we are and to take that as the raw material out of which we build a wonderful life. Our life, not someone else's. I don't have to be a concert pianist to play at parties. All I have to do is to love being the one who is able to play at parties.

April 17: Wisdom is the ability to select the best possible course in the worst possible moments. To pray for wisdom is to pray for the irresolvable elements of life and the talent to walk through land mines with snowshoes on.

April 18: Wisdom is what's left over after the experience has ended.

April 19: Everyone has something to teach us. That's why cultures before us revered the elderly so much. They have more to teach us about life than anyone else we know because they have lived it so much longer.

April 20: The function of frailty is to save us from self-righteousness — a far greater sin.

April 21: Never pretend to know what you do not. You will miss the chance to learn it from someone who really does.

April 22: Think of yourself as an hourglass with sand in it. The sand shifts at all times but it's never used up. It simply runs to begin again, over and over and over. Life is like that. What is happening to you now is not permanent. It is simply the process of learning one thing after another until life comes to fullness in you.

April 23: When we begin to understand that everything that happens to us teaches us something about what it means to be alive, we have learned all there is to learn in life. Then we can sit back and let God be in charge again.

April 24: To be "centered in wisdom" we have to lead a reflective life. We have to ask not only what is happening to us and the world around us but why it's happening and what should be done about its happening. The problem is that too many people simply go on going on, numbed out and unthinking. That's not life; that's vegetation.

April 25: "It is good to have an end to journey towards," Ursula Le Guin writes, "but it is the journey that matters in the end." How we get where we get is often more important in the end than getting there. The goodness of the work itself, the joy of the sharings while we do it and the love we find along the way, whether we succeed at it or not, now that's what makes life, life.

April 26: Fail? Of course we fail — if by "fail" you mean that we get lots of opportunities as we go through life to learn what we didn't want to know.

April 27: The point of life is not to succeed; it is to live it as well as we can. Even when we think we can't.

April 28: Self-acceptance depends on the ability to accept everybody else around us, just as they are, and still think neither less nor more about ourselves, knowing that who we are is for a purpose. God loves us as we are — weak, stumbling, and often unfaithful to our own highest ideals. Perhaps life is given to us so that we can learn to love ourselves as well. Otherwise, how can we ever find the God who dwells in us?

April 29: "If you wish to live, you must first attend your own funeral," Katherine Mansfield wrote. Put down your false expectations of yourself and remember that you will die. Then, go out and enjoy every minute of every day. You have absolutely nothing to lose now and nothing to fear.

April 30: There is such a thing as trying too hard. Be easy on yourself. When all is said and done, we will still be only human.

MAY

PSALM 52

*I am like
an olive tree,
growing in
the house of God.*

*L*ife is not about going through the motions from birth to death. Life is about the development of self to the point of unbridled joy. Life is about trusting our talents and following our gifts. But how? Olive trees hint at the answer even today.

Olive trees are a very important and very meaningful image in Jewish literature. To the Jewish mind, to grow "like an olive tree" is no small thing. It isn't easy to grow trees in the Middle East. Sand is hardly a conducive environment for forestry. Yet, there is one wood that seems to thrive on the difficulty of the process. There is one tree with a natural talent for life in the middle of nowhere. The olive tree grows hard wood on barren ground, with little water, for a long, long time.

To grow "like an olive tree," then, means to grow without much help, to grow hardy, to grow long, and to grow on very little nourishment. The olive tree doesn't need much to develop, it gives good wood at the end of a long, slow process of growth, and it doesn't die easily, sometimes not for thousands of years. The olive tree has a talent for life. There are some olive trees in the Garden of Olives, in fact, that scholars estimate were there the night of the Last Supper when Christ went there to pray. Startling, isn't it?

In this culture, in this age, on the other hand, the temptation is to think that everything — including our own natural abilities — ought to come easily. We want fast service and quick results. We want a lot for nothing. We want the greatest degree of return for the least amount of effort. And we want out of whatever doesn't work the first time. There is very little of the focused, the hardy, the persistent olive tree in us. There is very little talent for talent in us.

Yet talents that lie dormant in our souls destroy us from the inside out. If we do not learn to slowly, patiently, painfully, if necessary, let them come to life in us, we risk our own robotization. We give ourselves over to the pain of a living death. Talent is the gift that will not go away.

May 1: Have you ever known a person with a clear natural ability for music or languages who goes into math or science or business instead, and you wonder why? A talent is an ability natural to everyone but which exists in some people to an unusual degree and which, as a result, they often take for granted, discount, or consider too easy to really be worth anything. Talent can get lost when it's not recognized and encouraged. What you do well without thinking may be the very thing you should be doing with your life. The trick lies in being brave enough to trust the impulse to try.

May 2: Talent is not wisdom. It is not even knowledge, necessarily. Talent is raw gift. Wisdom comes in knowing how to use the talent well. And knowledge comes in the long, hard process of developing it. Talent is simply a formless waste of gold dust waiting to be molded. It's the long, hard process of shaping it that turns it into beauty.

May 3: To have a talent for gardening and not to develop it is to deprive the world of color. Imagine how gray the world would be if all the gardeners of the world never took flower growing seriously. The question is, Of what are we depriving the world?

May 4: It's not easy to be talented. It means having to accept ourselves for what we are instead of what we might prefer to be. Trying to bend a tree against the wind is not easy.

May 5: "Follow your bliss," Joseph Campbell wrote, "and you'll never work another day in your life." What you find blissful is probably your talent: furniture refinishing, auto repair, cake decorating, flower arranging, for instance. Why aren't you doing more of what is really important to you in life? Is your reason for not doing it a good one or simply an excuse not to have to make the effort to do the hard work that even talent requires?

May 6: There's a difference between an interest and a talent. It is important not to confuse the two. Just because I like something doesn't make me good at it. It may merely make me good at appreciating it. But then, appreciation may be a talent in itself.

May 7: Talent without the perseverance necessary to develop it is cheap. Too many people spend their lives talking about what they might have done — if they had only stayed at something long enough for it to bear fruit.

May 8: Doing well what must be done anyway is talent enough for anyone. Cleaning a room until it is really clean, fixing a chair so that it stays fixed, filing papers so that they can be found again — now those are talents that make the world beautiful.

May 9: To have a talent is to be obliged to use it. Talent is never given to us for our own sake.

May 10: To have talent implies being willing to fail over and over while we learn to succeed. Charles de Foucauld, the founder of the Little Brothers of Jesus, taught, "The absence of risk is a sure sign of mediocrity."

May 11: Talent is to be used for its highest possible purpose, to be a flash of light in a world that needs to see just one more foot ahead of itself.

May 12: Thoreau wrote, "In the long run we hit only what we aim at." Having the ability to do something is not the same as doing it.

May 13: Talent is creation made manifest. To use the talents we've been given is a godly act.

May 14: Vladimir Nabokov wrote with great insight, "Genius is an African who dreams up snow." Genius, in other words, always does the undoable. Don't be afraid of the new ideas that come from strange places. Sift every one of them carefully, but sift them all with the hope that comes from searching for diamonds in white sand.

May 15: Not everyone is a genius but everyone has talent, some piece of life that they do with great joy and better than they do anything else. We cannot leave the doing of our talents to someone else or they will never get done as we could have done them and the world will be forever unfinished. "Not a day passes over the earth, but men and women of no note do great deeds, speak great words, and suffer noble sorrows," Charles Reade wrote.

May 16: Talent touches the dark side of life as well as its dynamism. Too often one person's talent is another person's despair. Jealousy takes over where awe should be. When we measure ourselves by the people around us rather than the quality that we hold in trust within ourselves, we unleash the demons of hell into our own hearts. When you feel the clutch in your own heart at the sight of another person's abilities, ask yourself what it is that is begging to be developed in yourself that you have been neglecting. Nurture your own talent and you will not need to undermine someone else's.

May 17: It is when we want to be what we are not and fail to be the best of what we are that talent goes to seed and depression raises its hoary head in us. What a pathetic way to live.

May 18: "The principal mark of genius is not perfection but originality, the opening of new frontiers," Arthur Koestler wrote. If you're waiting to be perfect at something before you're willing to share its possibilities, you will still be waiting to do something of worth in this world three days after your own funeral.

May 19: "Genius," C. W. Ceram wrote, "is the ability to reduce the complicated to the simple." Be careful of what impresses you. Simply because a thing is obscure does not make it good. On the other hand, simply because a thing is clear does not make it worthless. Real intellectual talent is the ability to distinguish one from the other.

May 20: A talent is a predisposition to something, not a guarantee of anything. Talent must be fed and exercised and stretched and drained dry. Then, someday perhaps, for a single shining moment, it may burst into flame in one perfect picture, one perfect note, one perfect sentence, one perfect object, one perfect action, one perfectly radiant idea that breaks life open for someone else and makes it clear forevermore. At that moment, all the work will have been worth it.

May 21: "Talent is helpful in writing, but guts are absolutely necessary," Jessamyn West said. Talent requires the ability to try — and to fail. We look at people with talent and are in awe of their successes. It seldom occurs to us that they succeed only because they have been willing to fail so often.

May 22: If you are reading these reflections with sadness because of all the things in life you always wanted to do but never did, you have missed the point of the entire month. "It is never too late to be what you might have been," George Eliot said. Talent is that unsatisfied part of us that is dying to be developed and that, until it is, will lurk within us agitating and waiting to be recognized. If not by the world, at least by you. Go out this week and get whatever it is — the brushes, the chisels, the books, the camera, the kit, the lessons — that you need to begin what you have always wanted to do. Grandma Moses began to paint in her eighties. And, come to think of it, so did my aunt.

May 23: The other side of talent is industry. You have to want something enough to put limits on all the lesser things in life that are eating up your time and, worse, eating up your soul. Ask any housewife.

May 24: Talent is the unexpressed part of me, the part I'm dying to try and fear to attempt. "At my age?" we ask. "In my position?" "With my responsibilities?" Well, do you want to die happy? Then go ahead — try it.

May 25: As Josh Billings says: "Consider the postage stamp. It's usefulness consists in the ability to stick to one thing until it gets there." Don't give up. That little thing you consider worthless is what people look to you to do better than anyone else can do it. Give it your all. The world needs it.

May 26: Olive trees defy nature. They grow without a great deal of water. And they keep on growing and producing far beyond trees of more usual types. No talent comes to fullness in a day, but once developed it simply gets better and better. The problem is that you have to be willing to start what will necessarily be the long, dry process of turning what is possible into what is real.

May 27: Consider the abilities you resent in others. You're getting a clear message there: those things are either what you can do well and should be developing or what you can't do well and should let go of so that you can get on with who you really are instead of wishing your life away.

May 28: Antonio Salieri, Mozart's contemporary and rival, was a good musician but not a Mozart. Unfortunately, he couldn't accept being Salieri and died in agony, wishing he were what he was not. One of life's greatest talents is the ability to be the best we can be, to accept ourselves and to enjoy it.

May 29: Talent is what we develop; genius is what we do without trying. Genius is rare, but everyone has some talent of some kind.

May 30: Talent makes creation a divine impulse but a human affair.

May 31: Genius gives us a measure of human possibility; talent gives us an insight into the dizzying gift of life.

JUNE

PSALM 86

*Teach me
your ways
that I may walk
in your truth.*

*T*his month's psalm verse is a dangerous one. Think carefully before you pray it. God's ways, we have long been warned, are simply not our ways. Whatever this universe is about, it is not about anything we think is normal. Who of us would have thought to have made people of different colors? Who of us could have imagined the amoeba? Which one of us would have put stripes on fish and spots on dogs and flowers in deserts? No, God does not think the way we do.

Nor does God expect the same things of us that we too often do of one another. God does not expect perfection, or why would every living thing get an incalculable number of second tries? God does not expect total understanding, or why would life be one long learning process? God does not expect instant acquiescence, or why would there be such a thing as free will? God knows that life is a series of experiences meant to make us better able to handle the next one.

As life goes on, either we get to be more kind, more patient, and less exercised about the little things around us, or, it is apparent, we fail to grow into the ways of the God who is clearly kind, eternally patient, totally confident in the ultimate goodness of this flimsy thing called humanity.

To become what God wants us to be, however, we need to come to grips with a lot of things about ourselves along the way. It is, after all, what we think about ourselves that really determines what we think about other people. If we're secure and self-accepting, we understand others and are not threatened by them. If we feel inadequate and uncertain about ourselves, we can easily become jealous or intimidated by others — and blame them for it. Clearly, if we want to grow to be good for others — our families, our friends, all the people of the world whose lives are impacted by the vibrations in our own — we must someday come to accept the truth about ourselves.

June 1: Everything that bothers us about somebody else reveals to us something about ourselves. Impatience with the other demonstrates the irritability in us; criticism of the other marks the self-righteousness in us; indifference toward the other points out the self-centeredness in us. Those are the truths that must be confronted. For the sake of the other? Only partially. Most of all, we must confront the disquiets in ourselves for the sake of our own peace of soul.

June 2: "The sins of others are before our eyes; our own are behind our backs," the Roman poet Seneca wrote. The terrible truth has been spoken. We hide from others and from ourselves those things about ourselves which, if we knew them, could save us. If we admitted our arrogance, faced our dishonesties, named our weaknesses — at least to ourselves — we would be consumed with kindness. We would know what God knows: that there is no one who is not struggling with the same kinds of things we are. There is no one who does not need and deserve our care.

June 3: We resist God's ways with all our hearts and poison the present with resentment of change and attempts to control the future. Learning to accept the now with trust is one of life's greatest blessings.

June 4: It is a sad theology that concentrates only on God's commandments. When we forget about God's life alive in us, all we ever really know is how to be fearful, instead of how to be happy.

June 5: "Confession" is the process of placing before another the depth of my struggle to be fully human and of being surprised at how much that person loves me despite it. Self-revelation, in other words, is simply a dry run for judgment day. A very comforting dry run, indeed.

June 6: The only people worthy to be someone else's confessor are those who know their own weaknesses — and their own efforts to wrestle them to the floor of their hearts. Those people are kind.

June 7: When we ourselves discover who we really are, we have come to know what God knows. Now we are ready to begin.

June 8: The Chinese say, "There is my truth. There is your truth. There is the truth." All I can see is what is apparent from where I'm standing. If I want to know what a thing is really about, I must learn to listen to how it looks to someone else from where that person is standing in life. Then, I have to learn to say, "Yes, I see what you mean."

June 9: God gives us the ability to remember the past and experience the present. The future lies in darkness. Therefore, every day is another opportunity to come to new truth. It requires, of course, that we be open to it. Those people and institutions who live today as if only the truth of the past counted blindfold themselves to the ongoing ways of God. How sad.

June 10: Anything that cannot be questioned is a sin against the fertile mind of God. Thank God for Galileo; thank God for Martin Luther; thank God for feminists. Because of them the rest of us get the chance to see new life and God's life at work anew in us.

June 11: I love this one: The French philosopher Montaigne writes, "I speak the truth, not so much as I would, but as much as I dare; and I dare a little more, as I grow older." Watch out, world! Young rebels dedicated to new truths are society's most dangerous revolutionaries in their old age. They are too old to punish, too honest to ignore.

June 12: When we walk in God's truth all our lives, respectful of the role of institutions but never contained by them, we become more and more free, more and more candid every day of our lives. Maybe that's what accounted for John XXIII. He had walked in God's ways so long no lesser path could confine him.

June 13: The problem with truth is that it demands of us courage as well.

June 14: Josh Billings says, "It's not only the most difficult thing to know one's self, but the most inconvenient." Right: When I come to know myself I know what God's sense of humor is all about.

June 15: There may be nothing more painful than knowing who we are, true. But there's also nothing more liberating. Once we stop trying to be someone else, once we "walk in the way of God's truth" for us, life can begin. We can come out from behind all the cautions and all the masks and live.

June 16: Personal honesty confronts us with the truth of ourselves. Down deep we remember all the bad that's in us — and try to hide it. Even from ourselves. But there's no gain in that. The goal of life is to give more attention to growth than we do to guilt. The real function of guilt, surely, is to goad us to grow, not to leave us wallowing in fruitless pain.

June 17: "The ways of God" are the ways that lead us to the development of the divine in us. The point

of life is not to become perfect, as in fixed and finished and done. There is no such thing. The goal
of life is simply, at the end, to have the good in us
outweigh the dross.

June 18: The reason we seek self-knowledge is not
narcissism. The fact is that we cannot know where we
need to go next in life if we do not know where we
have been, what we have come through, where we fell
and when we soared. Those are the compass points of
growth, indicators of new ways forward, the markers
of our lives.

June 19: At twenty we have dreams and desires
to forge; at forty we have goals and achievements
to gain; at sixty if we have managed to remain true
to our highest ideals — whatever the cost, however
the squalls — we have the burning contentment, the
peaceful strength that comes with being worth more
inside than the sum total of everything we have
gained on the outside. Then nothing outside of us can
touch or shake or frighten us at all.

June 20: If we pray, "Teach us your ways, O God,"
we are going to have to expect the lessons. Be careful.
Are you really up to this?

June 21: Truth is not a constant. Truth is a volcano that turns last year's mountain into this year's plain. "The world is flat" was once geographical truth. "The earth is the center of the universe" was once theological certainty. "Women are property" was once a cultural creed. God showed us God's way and all these things shimmered into nothingness. Don't think for a moment that new truth isn't just as much at work right now as then, if God is still active in the universe and we are still but blind believers. No article of faith is a substitute for God.

June 22: "Those who believe in their truth...leave the earth behind them strewn with corpses," E. M. Cioran wrote. "Religions number in their ledgers more murders than the bloodiest tyrannies account for...." Be careful of your certainties. They may be your greatest sins. Unless, of course, the God who is One has told something different to every person on earth.

June 23: Max Lerner wrote: "The crime of book purging is that it involves a rejection of the word. For the word is never absolute truth, but only our frail and human effort to approach the truth. To reject the word is to reject the human search." To stamp out the attempts of others to come closer to the truth makes it impossible for everyone, in the long run, to walk in the truth because we will have refused to let it in, one small fragment of hope amid a profusion of falsehood.

June 24: The Zen say, "Sit, walk, or run — but don't wobble." Got it?

June 25: A Turkish proverb teaches: "If you speak the truth, have a foot in the stirrup." I think a loose translation of that little gem is either "Be prepared to follow the truth you teach" or "Be prepared to get out of town after you've taught it." Either interpretation is a valid one. Truth-tellers need to model what they say, but what they say will seldom be welcome at the outset because it upsets the unsayable. Truth-tellers have very small birthday parties.

June 26: Those who swallow a stone become a stone. What bothers us, what we don't work at until we come to peace with it, stops us in our living tracks. Then "truth" becomes a burden that suffocates us, preoccupies us, drains us of the energy that we need to go on from here. Trust someone with any secret that has become too heavy for you to carry alone. Choose that person wisely and selectively, of course, but for the sake of your future, choose.

June 27: Malcolm Muggeridge wrote, "It has been said that when human beings stop believing in God they believe in nothing. The truth is much worse: they believe in anything." Cling to God whatever the corruption of the state, the authoritarianism of the church, the fragility of the family, the perfidy of friends. In all those losses, one truth remains on which we can rely: God is. And that truth is enough.

June 28: Failure is the foundation of truth. It teaches us what isn't true, and that is a great beginning. To fear failure is to fear the possibility of truth. The problem with failure is not that it happened; the problem lies simply in continuing to defend it.

June 29: Lord Byron wrote: "Opinions are made to be changed — or how is truth to be got at?" Well, that idea makes sense to me, but how many people have you ever heard admit that they have changed their opinion? To be able to change when change is necessary is surely a mark of greatness. Maybe that's why it's so rare.

June 30: "Bear ye one another's burdens," Compline, the night prayer of the church, reminds us, "and so you will fulfill the Law of Christ." Put up with one another, take care of one another, learn from one another, and you will have done everything that life demands of you, the prayer implies. Those are the eternal truths of human community. Those are God's ways.

JULY

PSALM 130

*My soul
waits for you;
I count on
your word.*

*C*ommitment and enthusiasm are two concepts that are, unfortunately, often confused. Commitment is that quality of life that depends more on the ability to wait for something to come to fulfillment — through good days and through bad — than it does on being able to sustain an emotional extreme for it over a long period of time. Enthusiasm is excitement fed by satisfaction. The tangle of the two ideas, however, is exactly what leads so many people to fall off in the middle of a project. When the work ceases to feel good, when praying for peace gets nowhere, when the marriage counseling fails to reinvigorate the marriage, when the projects and the plans and the hopes worse than fail, they fizzle, that's when the commitment really starts. When enthusiasm wanes and romantic love dies and moral apathy — a debilitating loss of purpose and energy — sets in, that is the point at which we are asked to give as much as we get. That's when what we thought was an adventure turns into a commitment. Sometimes a long, hard, demanding one that tempts us to despair. As if God will ever abandon the good. As if waiting for God's good time were a waste of our time. As if God's Word of love will ever fail us in the end.

Once upon a time, the dove said to the cloud, "How many snowflakes does it take to break a branch?" "I have no idea," the cloud replied. "I simply keep on snowing until it does." "Mmmmm," the little dove mused. "I wonder how many voices it will take before peace comes?"

Commitment is that quality of human nature that tells us not to count days or months or years, conversations or efforts or rejections but simply to go on going on until "all things are in the fullness of time," until everything is ready, until all hearts are in waiting for the Word of God in this situation to be fulfilled.

When we feel most discouraged, most fatigued, most alone is precisely the time we must not quit.

July 1: "The greatest thing of all is caring," Friedrich von Hügel wrote. "Caring is everything." And he should know. Von Hügel, the lay theologian whose work helped to usher in the era of modern theology and scripture study, knew resistance on every side from the church he loved. Nevertheless, he persisted and his legacy lives on in us. By the way, even in the face of all that pressure, these were the last words he said. On his deathbed. Now that's commitment.

July 2: Commitment is not staying in a place from which you cannot leave. Commitment lies in working at a thing unceasingly, in never ceasing to work at it, no matter how bleak may become the prospect of ever bringing life to it again.

July 3: How do you know when you're really committed to something? Easy. When what happens to it still affects you, you are committed to it, whatever the discomfort of it all.

July 4: All commitments have their times of total unfeeling, times when we wonder why we ever loved this thing, this person, this group at all. Don't be afraid of those times. Those are the periods when we are busy finding ourselves again so that we will have new life to bring to what has drained every ounce from us already.

July 5: Disillusionment is the test of commitment. When we see a thing as it really is and yet continue to care about it, then we are dealing in more than a passing fancy. Then love has taken the place of what might otherwise have been only fad.

July 6: Commitment is hanging on, despite the fact that we have already let go. When a thing ceases to give life to you, it may be time for *you* to start giving life to you.

July 7: I don't know how to break this to you: Commitment is not burning passion. It is the serious business of going on even though the party has long been over.

July 8: When you cease to care about something that once was the center of your life, ask yourself if it says something about it — or something about you. The answer to that question has a great deal to tell you about what you need to do next.

July 9: Without commitment, life turns to cotton in the mouth.

July 10: The purpose of life is to be about something greater than ourselves.

July 11: Mae West said once, "Too much of a good thing is wonderful." How freeing. Commitment, that insight implies, is the ability to go overboard for something. If you're not unbalanced about something in life, you haven't begun to live.

July 12: It is so easy to commit ourselves to the winning side. What really counts, however, is to commit ourselves to what isn't winning — but should be.

July 13: Don't be afraid to say your tentative truth. It may awaken someone else's truth, as well. And the truth we see that is yet to be is the raw material of commitment.

July 14: It's not easy to keep our energy up when there's no energy left, true. But real commitment is the stuff that runs on air, not energy.

July 15: Commitment is refusing to quit a cause that has already — apparently — lost.

July 16: If you attend only to what is, you will never achieve what should be.

July 17: Inspiration is what it takes to get us started. Commitment is what it takes to keep us going.

July 18: Never count success in terms of the number of people who begin a project. Just ask yourself how many people, if any, will be left after everyone else has gotten sensible and left.

July 19: Sometimes we start something good without knowing where it will end. That's when counting on the Word of God makes co-creators of us all.

July 20: Don't give up — at least not until they start taking animals to the Kennedy Space Center two by two.

July 21: Commitment is staying with the first invitation even when the second one is more exciting.

July 22: Counting on God's commitment to us is what makes possible our commitment to everything else.

July 23: Commitment and masochism are not synonyms. Sometimes commitment to the Word of God demands that we leave that we have already begun so that real life can come to fullness in us.

July 24: Commitment is the fine art of waiting for a thing to become for us what we thought a long time ago that it was.

July 25: There is nothing more boring than the person who is too sophisticated to care. You know the kind: the ones with the drooped eyelids who yawn when you tell them that California just dropped into the sea.

July 26: Apathy is what happens when there's no life left in the commitment. What has no life for us renders us lifeless. The secret, of course, lies in bringing to lost lives what they can no longer bring to us.

July 27: Apathy, indifference, listlessness are often simply the countersigns of adulthood. Children wait for someone else to satisfy them. Adults are people who are able to make their own happiness. To find nothing in anything is often because we put nothing into everything.

July 28: "Science may have found a cure for most evils," Helen Keller wrote, "but it has found no remedy for the worst of them all — the apathy of human beings." Most of the problems on earth are solvable. The problem is not that we don't have the technological skill. The problem is that we don't have the political will. Which translated means that you and I don't really care enough yet to demand a solution. Name three things to which you are committed. Name one thing you did this year to make them happen.

July 29: The psychiatrist Rollo May teaches that hate is not the opposite of love, that apathy is. What we hate is at least still worth enough to us to arouse in us an intense human response. Indifference to something means that it doesn't matter to us at all, has become invisible, is not worth our care, has been reduced to nothingness in us. Is there any worse fate than that? Ask yourself to whom or to what you are indifferent. That will tell you to whom or to what you are committed.

July 30: Dante makes the moral difference between commitment and apathy very plain. He wrote: "The hottest places in hell are reserved for those who, in time of great moral crisis, maintain their neutrality." The question for us in our time, of course, is about which of life's great crises have we chosen to be neutral when the lives of many depend on our commitment.

July 31: "If you stand for something important, write it in big bold letters so that someone can see it," the

Greek philosopher Socrates taught. Which translated means stop kidding yourself. If your favorite line is, "Of course I agree. I just think it's very important not to upset people with these new notions of pollution controls, universal human rights, ecology, and feminism," that's not commitment; that's politics.

AUGUST

PSALM 46

*Be still
and know that
I am God.*

Two images surround this month's theme of Sabbath and leisure for me. The first memory lies buried in old poetry, the second in a rabbi whose name I cannot remember.

The first incident happened during my first year of high school, I think. I had somehow stumbled onto the works of the French poet Charles Péguy, who wrote, "I love the one who sleeps, says God." The words didn't mean much to me at the time; if anything they seemed a little silly or, at the very least, confusing. But, interestingly enough, those words have stayed with me every year since. Now, decades of monastic life later, I have come to understand the wisdom of them, I have begun to realize their importance. Sleep, I now understand, is a sign of trust. The ability to rest gives the world back to God for a while. Rest, Sabbath, leisure all release a part of us that the corsets of time and responsibility every day seek to smother and try to suppress.

The second incident happened during a trip to Jerusalem years later. A local rabbi had joined us for the meal that celebrated the opening of Shabbat. I remember, for obvious reasons, as if it were yesterday, his final example of the perfect Sabbath observance. "You see this?" he said, taking a pen out of his breast pocket and twirling it in his fingers. "I am a writer and on the Sabbath I never allow myself to carry a pen. On the Sabbath I must allow myself to become new again."

In those two moments, I discovered what the psalmist tries to teach us in Psalm 46 about learning to be still. It is more than the simple observation that everyone needs to let go a little, to get rested enough to work harder next week, to change pace from the hectic to the chaotic. It is far beyond the fact that everyone needs a vacation. Oh no, it is much more than that. What this month's psalm verse teaches us is the simple truth that a soul without a sense of Sabbath is an agitated soul.

August 1: The first reason for the Sabbath, the rabbis teach, is to equalize the rich and the poor. Safe from the threat of labor on the Sabbath, the poor lived for at least one day a week with the same kind of freedom that the rich enjoyed. The Sabbath, in other words, is God's gift to the dignity of all humankind. It forces us to concentrate on who we are rather than on what we do.

August 2: The second reason for the Sabbath, the rabbis say, is to lead us to evaluate our work. As God did on the seventh day, we are also asked to determine whether or not what we are doing in life is really "good." Good for ourselves, good for the people around us, good for the development of the world. But if that is true, then the reason we have nuclear bombs and pornographic movies and underpaid workers may be precisely because we have lost respect for the concept of Sabbath. I mean, how long has it really been since you sat down, thought about what your life is about, and asked yourself if the work you do is really, really "good" work?

August 3: The third reason for the Sabbath, the Hebrew tradition teaches us, is very unlike the American compulsion to turn Sunday into more of the same only louder, faster, and longer. Sabbath is to lead us to reflect on life itself — where we've been, where we're going, and why. Sabbath time takes quiet and serious thought and a search for meaning.

August 4: How long has it been since you've taken a day simply to reflect on the way you live life — how fast, how balanced, how sensible, how realistic is it? The sad thing is that too often we choose to fret about life rather than reflect on it. We choose to worry about what might happen next instead of deciding what it is that should happen next.

August 5: Let's see now: If God built rest into the human cycle for 1 day out of every 7, or 52 days a year, or 3640 days in the average life-span of 70 years, or about 10 years out of every lifetime, I'm confused. Tell me again: Why are you tired?

August 6: Play and holy leisure are not the same things. We need both. Real play is purposeless activity that frees us to function in the world without concern for roles and obsession with results. Holy leisure consists of those activities that deepen the meaning of life. "Leisure," Cicero says, "consists in all those virtuous activities by which we grow morally, intellectually, and spiritually. It is that which makes a life worth living."

August 7: In ancient times, play was built right into the public calendar. That's what holidays and feast days were about. People worked daily from first light to last. Except on the feasts of the church, which were devoted to play and celebration. Play and Sabbath were two different parts of life. Play was recreating, imaginative, and socially inclusive, but the Sabbath was reserved for holy leisure, for reflection on the Word of God and its application to personal life.

August 8: Now people work so hard at play and find such little personal meaning in their work that they often bring neither physical rest nor spiritual renewal to the beginning of every new week.

August 9: Too often we resent our work as an interruption of our lives instead of seeing it as our part in the process of creation. But for that insight to occur we would have to remember again the purpose of Sabbath in the human enterprise.

August 10: Never think for a moment that silence is the absence of noise. Silence simply enables us to hear the noise inside ourselves rather than continue to contribute to the noise outside ourselves.

August 11: Silence is that vehicle for the messages of the soul which emerge in Sabbath-time and enrich all the rest of time as well.

August 12: The Japanese say, "One cannot learn to swim in a field." If you want something to happen, the proverb implies, you have to go where it can. But if that's the case, then we may really have a problem. Wisdom is the fruit of reflection. Reflection is the task of the Sabbath.

August 13: A culture that prefers the raucous to the reflective can't expect to produce wisdom figures in profusion. Maybe that's why we have more Butthead than Bach, more gunpowder than food stamps in this country.

August 14: Are we more responsible and important people — just because we rush everywhere?

August 15: The temptation is to confuse holy leisure and idleness. In idleness, nothing goes in and nothing comes out. We stare into space and space stares back. In holy leisure, we open our minds to all the beauty of life, invade ourselves with ideas, and become more beautiful ourselves in the process.

August 16: Lewis Mumford writes, "A society that gives to one class all the opportunities for leisure, and to another all the burdens of work, dooms both classes to spiritual sterility." Think of that one in a world where people are working two jobs at once and are still poor nevertheless. That's called social sin and someday somebody is going to have to answer for it.

August 17: "Sunday clears away the rust of the whole week," Joseph Addison wrote in *The Spectator*. Unless, of course, we mistake inertia for re-creation and simply use Sunday to become more waterlogged by work or idle activity than we were before it.

August 18: To become something new we must consciously do something different from what we have been doing before this. Try it next Sunday. See if Monday is a better experience because of it.

August 19: "Anybody can observe the Sabbath," Alice Walker said, "but making it holy surely takes the rest of the week." Now there's a thought. Going to church on Sunday and being self-righteous, ruthless, and judgmental the rest of the week may not be compatible behaviors. Imagine the number of things that could be ruined if that idea ever got around.

August 20: If there's nothing you do in life that you don't have time to do, you may well be wasting your life. Think about it.

August 21: Enjoying life and wasting it are two different things. The difference lies in what each of them does to the center of us. One fills us up; the other empties us out.

August 22: "Money and time are the heaviest burdens of life," Samuel Johnson wrote, "and...the unhappiest of all mortals are those who have more of either than they know how to use." Everything has a purpose far beyond itself. The celebration of the Sabbath is designed to help us determine how to use both well.

August 23: Unemployment is not idleness, and it is not Sabbath. It is the misuse of a person's initiative, the slow annihilation of the human soul. The multitude of people from every class of life who, against their will, have been displaced in this country know the loss of self-esteem and the social stigma that comes with being useless, lazy, inept. The real disease, however, may lie not in the fact that these people have failed the system but that the rest of us have failed to engage in the kind of reflection that the Sabbath calls for.

August 24: Have we really been better off as people, as families, as a nation since we began to shop on Sundays too? Maybe yes, maybe no.

August 25: Leisure has no value in itself besides whatever values we fill it with.

August 26: The sign of a life gone berserk is a life without weekends, without those moments when work stops and other things — like family and reading and gardening and the arts and quiet talks on important subjects — go far into the night.

August 27: Be careful what you fill your life with when your life is supposedly being filled with good things. The quality of our leisure defines the quality of our lives.

August 28: How many new activities, ideas, and experiences have you filled your life with lately — or are you at that point in life where all you do is what you always do? How long has it been since you've been dead — and has anybody noticed?

August 29: To become something new we need to allow ourselves — propel ourselves — into doing new things. It doesn't just happen.

August 30: The purpose of leisure is to give us the time to experiment with being the rest of the person that we have yet to be.

August 31: Look at it this way: If you're afraid of doing strange things, you are simply going to get even stranger doing the same old things for the rest of your life. Dullness is not a virtue.

SEPTEMBER

PSALM 16

The lot marked out
for me is my delight;
welcome indeed
the heritage
that falls to me.

I grew up on fairy tales and fables. I remember with special affection the story of "Goldilocks and the Three Bears." As a small child I was mesmerized by its structure and repetition — "This porridge is just right," I would sing with Goldilocks over and over again — but it was only as an adult that I came to appreciate the value of the story. It may not have been great poetry, true. But I have come to understand that it was, nevertheless, a piece of profound philosophy, a study in good psychology, an example of ancient and great spirituality. The writer of Psalm 16 would have liked "Goldilocks and the Three Bears," too, I think.

We live in a culture that conspires against us. Every day advertising agencies tell us that we need just one more thing to be truly happy. We need to do one more thing, they advise us, if we want to be really successful. We need to achieve one more thing in our lives, they insist, if we are to be totally valuable people. Hardly anyone ever tells us that we're fine just the way we are — thin or hefty, introverted or extroverted, shy or sociable. So we spend our lives trying to reshape ourselves or, barring that, trying to hide the shape we're in from the gaze of those who know from the same ads what it is we're lacking. Nothing is ever "just right."

It's the sense of lack that depresses us.

It's the awareness of inadequacy that leaves us feeling disadvantaged.

It's the absence of satisfaction with ourselves that drives us to measure ourselves by those around us — and find ourselves deficient.

The ancients called the failure to pursue the things of God or to recognize the obstacles to union with God in our own lives "spiritual blindness." And that it surely is. But it is just as surely true that failing to recognize the stuff of union with God that lies within us is spiritual blindness as well.

Psalm 16 calls us to be what we are with full confidence that it is precisely in the configuration of qualities that we call "ourselves" that we will find the God who is leading us to their fullness. Running away from ourselves, no matter how well intentioned, becomes instead a flight from the spiritual life. Then, after we have worked so hard to be richer, thinner, faster, and louder, we wonder how it is that we can have everything — and still feel empty.

September 1: "We are all worms," Winston Churchill said, "but I do believe that I am a glow-worm." Believing that we have what it takes to live a wonderful life is an essential part of living a wonderful life.

September 2: The time we spend measuring ourselves against someone else is time taken away from being what we ourselves are meant to be. That is a great loss, not just for ourselves, but for those who need what we alone can give.

September 3: "Jealousy is...a tiger that tears not only its prey but also its own raging heart," Michael Beer wrote. What we want outside our "allotted portion" — to such an extent that we lose sight of what we do have for the sake of what we can't have — will eventually sicken our own soul.

September 4: Aspiration, ambition, and jealousy are not the same things. Aspiration motivates us to be the best of what we are, ambition drives us to be more than we are, and jealousy plunges us into refusing to acknowledge that someone else is what we want to be and are not. Aspiration leads to greatness; ambition and jealousy debauch the heart.

September 5: The beauty of life does not lie in what we have or what we do. It lies in what we are and what we think while we're doing it. When asked what job he did, the first worker said, "I lay stones." But when the next worker was asked the same question, he said with pride, "I build cathedrals." It isn't what other people think of what we do that counts. It's what we think of what we do that makes the difference.

September 6: If the "normal" body is the anorexic or the muscle-bound figures we see on TV and in clothing ads, will somebody please tell me why we see so few of that kind walking around?

September 7: One of the synonyms for "delight" is "fascination." That's the translation of Psalm 16 I would prefer. Imagine what would happen to our souls if we prayed, "The lot marked out for me fascinates me" — as in intrigues me or tantalizes me or beguiles me into wondering what surprise lies for me behind this strangely packaged gift of God called my life.

September 8: We don't have to want what is happening to us right now. The psalmist tells us simply to welcome it, to let it in, to live it through, to walk with trust down dark paths knowing that light is not the only dimension that defines the stretch of day.

September 9: "When you are aspiring to the highest place, it is honorable to reach the second or even the third rank," Cicero tried to teach us. When we see people who are disappointed with silver medals in Olympic competition, it ought to be a sign to us that as a culture we are warping our hearts with goals that are paltry and plebeian.

September 10: "After the game, the king and pawn go into the same box," an Italian proverb reads. When all is said and done, we all have the same resources within us with which to play the game of life. What we too often fail to realize is that the game of life is actually played inside a person, not outside of us at all. Or to put it another way: I've known some very happy bag ladies and some very sour CEOs. You figure it out.

September 11: When you cannot have what you think you would enjoy, you must learn to enjoy what you have or you will wish your life away while roses die at your feet.

September 12: Antoine de Saint-Exupéry wrote: "To live is to be slowly born." We discover life and who we are in it one day at a time. No one ever has it all at once. No one.

September 13: Every day we run the exhilarating risk of living better than we did the day before. All we have to do is to deal with each incident as a challenge to be achieved rather than a crisis to be survived.

September 14: Each of us is capable of so much and no more, of this but not that, of becoming but not achieving. Knowing that is the secret of interior peace.

September 15: "No bird soars too high, if it soars with its own wings," the poet William Blake wrote. It's trying to be somebody else, in other words — the pretty sister, the athletic brother, the wealthy neighbor, the sought-after friend, which will, in the end, mark the low tide of life for us.

September 16: Every person alive is given a piece of the planet to cultivate and cherish. It's when we neglect what we can do in order to pursue what we can't do that we breed in ourselves the unhappiness that suffocates the soul.

September 17: When you find yourself wanting what someone else has — a position, a talent, a reputation, a lifestyle — ask yourself then why it is that being who you are, what you are, and where you are is not enough for you. What is missing in you that fuels a false hope? Sometimes it is simply the fact that we know there is more in us than we have yet to express. That is the grace of aspiration. At other times, it is because we know that we are not what we want to be and so we resent anyone who is. That is ambition gone awry.

September 18: "Do what you can, with what you have, where you are," Theodore Roosevelt wrote. There is struggle everywhere. The grace of life is to choose the one of which we are capable.

September 19: We cannot wish ourselves into realities not our own. We can only accept them and strive to make them better.

September 20: To spend life trying to be what I am not turns the poetry of life into prose too obscene to be printed. Imagine how barren it must be to die wanting to have been something I was not while whatever I was never came to fullness because I myself failed to value it.

September 21: People who are jealous of other people's gifts are in the wrong field. If you fall in that category of people who want to be more than they are, move quickly to develop another interest before you find out that you spent your entire life in the wrong arena.

September 22: "The lure of the distant and the difficult is deceptive. The great opportunity is where you are," John Burroughs wrote. Maybe. But the distant — where responsibilities cease and opportunities lie unbounded by the realities that lurk within us and the people that exist around us — is so much more alluring, isn't it? That's what you call fantasy.

September 23: There's a Hindustani proverb that reads: "Pearls are of no value in a desert." Right. And neither are oysters. Effective people give everything they have to the task before them. They don't wish it away or shirk it or blame it or complain about it. They just do it — as well as they can. And then they sit and reap the rewards that come to people who are totally themselves.

September 24: Have you heard about the optimist who, while falling from the top of a ten-story building, shouted at each floor, "I'm all right so far. And the view is terrific." Trust me: it's an attitude to be cultivated. After all, what is to be gained by worrying all the way down when you can, at least, enjoy the ride.

September 25: Pessimists poison an atmosphere. Nothing is ever good enough for them. Those are the people you stop inviting to Thanksgiving dinner.

September 26: Oscar Wilde may have said it best when he wrote, "A pessimist is one who when he has a choice of two evils, chooses both." And then projects them onto the rest of humankind. Who needs it?

September 27: Chasing after the dreams of a consumer society turns people into plastic robots — thinner than they should be, harder working than they ought to be, more in debt than they want to be, and less successful than they could be if they would simply do what they want to do and do it as well as they are able to do it.

September 28: Some people die without ever having known themselves because they have been too busy trying to be someone else. In which case, what is creation all about? If God wanted us all to be alike, why would each one of us be different? Tell someone in your own field today how good they are in their work.

September 29: "Thou shalt not covet" is the commandment many people pay no attention to. As a result, many people are miserable.

September 30: "This porridge is too hot," said Goldilocks. "This porridge is too cold," she said. "But this porridge is just right," said Goldilocks. And God looked at Goldilocks — and laughed with delirious delight.

OCTOBER

PSALM 19

Day after day
takes up the story;
night after night
makes known the message.

*T*he past is not where we live. Those who cling to it — either its joys or its pains — deny themselves the possibilities of the present. At the same time, those who are not nourished by the past deny themselves good measure by which to build a new future. Wherever we are today, the past is some explanation for it. But the past is no reason to continue anything in the present unless there is still enough energy in it to make what we are doing today necessary, worthwhile. Generation after generation we tell ourselves the stories of the past, the tasks of the present and the promise of the future. Each of them is measured by the eternal truths in the human heart, the call of God that rumbles through the world. This tension between past experience, the wisdom of the ages, and the underlying urgency of now leaves us with the spiritual balancing act of all time. Lord Halifax wrote, "Education is what remains after we have forgotten all we have been taught." It is the need for change that challenges tradition, and it is tradition that makes change without apocalypse possible. What is left over after the process concludes itself is called life. Balancing the two is like walking a greased tightrope over Niagara Falls.

October 1: Tradition is not rigid adherence to the behaviors of the past. Tradition is loving adherence to the values of the past. It is precisely a respect for tradition that requires us to make whatever changes are necessary to keep foundational values as present today as once they were in the past. Just because Jesus walked from one place to another curing the sick, associating with outcasts, does not require us to walk from one place to another too. What is required is simply that we continue to care for the infirm, that we refuse to substitute self-righteousness for inclusion, whatever it takes to do that.

October 2: Tradition is the glue of a community. Think about that one for awhile.

October 3: To give an example: Tradition is what keeps a family coming together on Thanksgiving when, without it, warring brothers and sisters would never want to be in the same room together again for as long as they lived. It keeps us in contact until we're finally ready to discover how much we love one another.

October 4: Most of the things they taught me in the novitiate didn't make the remotest impression on me at the time. I did things simply because they were required of me. It was years later when I finally understood that there are many things in life that don't make sense until they make sense. The Rule of Benedict says to "follow the example of the elders." Now I understand why.

October 5: "It is not that I belong to the past," Mary Antin wrote, "but that the past belongs to me." People who try to trap us in the past do it to avoid facing the challenges of the present. Things like that happen when what we do becomes more important to us than why we do it.

October 6: To cut a person off from the past makes a god of the present. A false god.

October 7: The most difficult element in social change is helping people to distinguish the immediate past from the past. "We've always done it this way," is usually a synonym for "We've been doing this for the last fifty or a hundred years." And that's a very short time in the light of eternity.

October 8: A Chinese proverb teaches: "To know the road ahead, ask those coming back." Those who cut off the memory of a group too often cut off its future too. If you resist the guidance of those who went before you, ask yourself why it is that you need to have all the answers. And worse, all the questions too?

October 9: "If you want things to stay as they are," Giuseppe di Lampedusa wrote, "things will have to change." If you want the kind of family life you had in a small town, you will have to figure out what private traditions to substitute in a big city for Sundays at Gramma's and horseshoe throwing contests. You see, it's not Sunday dinner and family contests that count; it's family routines and family activities — whatever form they take in a new place at a new time — that maintain the sense of identity and acceptance we remember in years to come. It's the traditions we build together that keep us together when there is little obvious reason to continue.

October 10: What we have learned about life in the past is what we wrestle with in the present. What traditions were you raised on that mean the most to you now?

October 11: Things like male dominance and white power and female subordination are not "tradition," though many a religious figure of the past once argued so. They are simply long-lasting social practices which, based on bad biology, became theology as time went by. These must now give sway to new information and enlightened understanding. Otherwise, bleeding a person would still be basic medical practice, the sun would still revolve around the earth, Indians would still be half-souled, and church government would still be the law of the land because once we thought those things were part of the natural law. To blame God for things of human design, to call "revelation" what are simply long-lived practices derived on the basis of limited data is the worst "tradition" of them all.

October 12: "The first act of creation is destruction," the poet e. e. cummings wrote. Change is often traumatic, unwanted, unacceptable. Yet, all of them — death, the loss of a job, divorce — do in the end free us to begin again, to create our lives anew. Not everybody gets that opportunity.

October 13: Tradition is meant to be created anew, every single day. Otherwise, tradition becomes a rut instead of the ongoing revelation of God through every time in every people.

October 14: Tradition is meant to help us identify what is sacred in life — not to ossify it but to maintain it.

October 15: Anthony de Mello wrote, "A society that domesticates its rebels has gained its peace. But it has lost its future." When we use tradition to smother thought, the tradition loses its power to persuade and thought goes to straw. People with old ideas and a big club are not capable of building the future.

October 16: We try so hard to control life, to nail one foot of it to the ground, to stop it from turning on us, to deter the God of surprises — and so often we call that "tradition" instead of what it really is: fear.

October 17: When we sacralize practice and call it "tradition," we take the Holy Spirit out of the church.

October 18: Living in the past does not glorify the God of the present. Come to think about it, living in the future doesn't either.

October 19: "Tradition," G. K. Chesterton wrote, "means giving votes to the most obscure of all classes — our ancestors. It is the democracy of the dead. Tradition refuses to submit to the small and arrogant oligarchy of those who merely happen to be walking around." We are not the beginning and end of all truth. We may have more data, more facts, more science than past generations, but we do not necessarily have more wisdom, more insight, more awareness of the implications of what we do. The future depends on our dialoging with the past.

October 20: "A precedent embalms a principle," Benjamin Disraeli wrote. Before eliminating old practices it is imperative that we discover their purpose, not to justify keeping old practices but to guarantee that we do not lose what they were meant all along to teach us.

October 21: Beware of having to have a reason for doing everything your directors ask you to do. If an action is amoral, it at least deserves a try. After all, it is so easy to use "reason" as a way to avoid wisdom. Sometimes we have to do a thing a while in order to find out if there is any reason for doing it in our own lives. Children see no reason to be silent, to go to bed early, to learn to wait, but those are all qualities, nevertheless, that stand us in very good stead as the years go by. Go ahead, trust someone else's experience for a change. Take a walk in the woods of the soul — and find the new flowers there.

October 22: The wisdom of the ages never dies. It doesn't have to be cemented in the present by anachronisms from the past. It will emerge whether we want it to or not. The only question is how we choose to learn it — by running with it or running into it. As the psalmist teaches, "Day after day takes up the story; night after night makes known the message." It's a matter of being attuned to it.

October 23: Archbishop John Roach wrote in 1991, "The test of every institution or policy is whether it enhances or threatens human life and dignity." That and that alone is more than test enough of the difference between holy tradition and the barnacles of time. What is really God's will always enhances life. Or, at least, so Jesus taught when he broke one tradition after another that suppressed it for those considered "outcast."

October 24: The day the future is tied down by the past, life ceases to be real.

October 25: Change tests tradition. Any tradition that can't absorb change could not have been tradition in the first place.

October 26: Here's an idea: Write down four things that you do every year. Then, write down why you do them and what you get out of them. That's holy tradition. Yours.

October 27: Tradition enables change. Change is what tests the principles of tradition. One without the other is false.

October 28: "The tragedy of life is that people do not change," Agatha Christie wrote. I'm convinced that's true. I'm also convinced, however, that it is just as much a tragedy when they do change — without being grounded in the past, without a sense of purpose for the future.

October 29: "Most of us are about as eager to be changed as we were to be born," James Baldwin wrote, "and we go through our changes in a similar state of shock." Think about it for a minute. The womb was a tradition too. Too bad we didn't learn then how it is that the purpose of tradition is to carry us securely to the next step, not to hold us back.

October 30: We have two choices every day of our lives: to live a little more fully or to die a little more surely. When we pit tradition against change, our spirits atrophy from sclerosis of the heart. When we pit change against tradition, our souls shatter from the purposeless force of spastic energy.

October 31: The function of Christianity is not to preserve the past but to change the present in the light of the future.

NOVEMBER

PSALM 34

*Do not yield to evil
but embrace goodness.
Seek and strive
for lasting peace.*

The word "evil" is very little in use these days. Of all taboo words, this one is apparently least politically correct of the lot of them. We make "mistakes," we tell ourselves. We fail to live up to our "potential," perhaps. We even sometimes "hurt" other people and other things — the planet, for instance, minorities, of course, women as a class everywhere — because of "bad judgment" or "cultural training" or "poor information," but one thing we know for sure: we are certainly not "evil" people. True. I believe that. But I also believe that evil does exist.

There is no doubt in my mind that most adverse behavior is unwitting, unconscious, and inadvertent — done out of massive weakness or serious pressure or deep desperation. There is also no doubt, I think, that evil — conscious and willful destruction, dark and rancid ill will — does exist. How else do we explain rape hotels in Bosnia, a holocaust in Germany, industrial slavery in every part of the world? The question is, Where does it come from? What feeds it? What nurses it to monstrous proportions? What is it that lies in the center of the human heart waiting to destroy? What is it to which, if we yield, we run the road of mean-mindedness that makes all matter of human spoilage possible? The psalmist gives us a clue: it is the evil at war within our very selves, our personal selves, our private selves that makes social depravity possible. It is the disposition to envy, jealousy, turmoil that comes out of self-loathing. It leads us to battle with the universe in debilitating attempts to become what we are not. It is inner turmoil run rampant in the human soul that demonstrates itself by the destruction of others.

Internal peace and self-acceptance, then, is the antidote to evil. Jealousy, the sustained refusal to acknowledge the value and talent and power and strength and public affirmation of the other, is its mortal enemy. The evil done by jealousy is first of all done to ourselves because it eats away at us like acid in a battery. Disgusted with ourselves, we seek to repair the problem at someone else's expense. It is not a pretty picture. It is the beginning of evil. The implication is, of course, that we must free ourselves from ourselves before we can begin to free anyone else.

November 1: A Japanese proverb teaches: "When everyone praised the peacock for its beautiful tail, the birds cried with one consent, 'But look at its legs, and what a voice!'" People who build themselves up by tearing other people down are simply standing on the street corners of life shouting out their sense of personal inadequacy. Pity them. Most of all, don't listen to them.

November 2: The task of life is to become the best of what each of us is able to be, not to become someone else. Fresh, firm onions in a mushroom patch have a very special value.

November 3: The clue to whether or not jealousy is a seed in the center of me is not whether or not I have ever done anything to obstruct another person's climb to success. It is whether or not I can stand to hear another person praised in my presence. In that case, the problem is not with the other. It lies with the fact that there is something in me that I have either failed to develop or refused to accept.

November 4: To go through life wanting to be someone else must be a terrible burden. It is hard enough just learning to be myself.

November 5: The question is not whether or not I am capable of being a concert pianist. The question is whether or not I love music enough to love tuning the piano for the person who is.

November 6: Jealousy is vinegar in the soul. It withers the human spirit.

November 7: The English say, "When the proud hear another praised, they feel themselves injured." If we have our own joy in life, we don't need to have someone else's. The feat is to remember that we make joy; we don't get it for nothing.

November 8: Jealousy over things poisons a person's sense of worth; jealousy over people is worse. When we become jealous of the people we love, we set out to cage and tame exactly the spirit we first admired, not for their sake, but for ours.

November 9: Why choose to be jealous of another rather than supportive of their success? What can jealousy possibly do to us except make us miserable?

November 10: Jealousy destroys the very thing it sets out to protect: my own sense of well-being.

November 11: In the Decalogue there's one commandment about stealing, one about lying, one about murder, one about worship, one about God, one about blasphemy, and two about jealousy. Think about it. Somebody clearly knows something we don't know about what constitutes the corrosion of life.

November 12: A consumer society breeds jealousy and depends on it for its energy. Advertising, in fact, is geared to creating it. *Vogue Living* (Australia, October/November 1996) presents a skin product under a banner head that reads: "Make Your Friends Insanely Jealous." What we don't have we can't live without, they insist. Ask anyone who can afford the $200 soap dish they present on a preceding page. They're wrong. What we gain outside ourselves will never, ever make up for what we lack inside ourselves — that sense of personal satisfaction that makes life an adventure rather than a competition.

November 13: It is what we are free of desiring, not what we envy, that makes for human happiness.

November 14: Envy can, of course, help us to set a course in life. But, at the same time, envy can just as easily drive us in the wrong direction. Wanting what we cannot have or cannot do can only distract us from what we really should be doing.

November 15: Be careful of people who love you jealously. It's really themselves they love. You are simply a trophy to their need for power and control.

November 16: Groups that cannot support the talented in their midst are groups doomed to the eventual atrophy that comes with the homogenization of people.

November 17: The problem with jealousy is not so much that it springs from envy of another but that it is satisfied only with destruction of the other. What it cannot have for itself, it sets out to obstruct in others. The end result is the glorification of the mediocre.

November 18: Do you want to know if you yourself are struggling with jealousy? When introducing your friends to other people, do you point out their gifts to others or do you seek instead to conceal them? And if so, what is that saying about your own needs?

November 19: What we allow ourselves to envy, we will look for an excuse to destroy. The problem is that the damage we do is far more often to the fiber of ourselves than to the quality of the other — as Germany discovered with its destruction of the Jews.

November 20: Beware those who have something negative to say about everything. They are saying it about you too.

November 21: The secret of internal peace is the cultivation of the ability to let things go. When you lose something, say, "Oh, well. It's not the end of the world." When you break something, say, "Oh, well. It's not the end of the world." When you want something and fail to achieve it, say, "Oh, well. It's not the end of the world." Why? Because, you may be surprised to discover, it isn't. The only thing that is the end of the world is the end of the world.

November 22: "Freedom's just another word for nothing left to lose," Janis Joplin sang. Give something away today. Giving not only benefits the receiver; it benefits us. Giving begins the stripping down process that frees the heart and makes envy impossible. This may be a lot harder for you than you expected. Think about that for awhile.

November 23: "I envy paranoids," Susan Sontag wrote. "They actually feel people are paying attention to them." Envy is wanting something which you think will give you status or respect or control. But the fact is that even if we got it, very few people would really notice it. Which means that we would then need to get something else to get their attention. It's an exhausting circle and it spins interminably.

November 24: Take careful note of what you criticize in another person. It may be exactly what you want in yourself and have failed to develop.

November 25: Jealousy and envy are not necessarily the same thing. Jealousy is pathological rejection of the talents or gifts of another. Envy is the recognition that someone has had an opportunity that I am entitled to but have not been given. Envy can well be a signal of an injustice that needs to be righted. Girls envied boys their good educations, their good jobs, their good salaries. People reduced by our society to social welfare often envy those who are not. In those cases, the evil lies in letting the injustice go unnamed and unchallenged.

November 26: Beware what you envy; you may get it.

November 27: A jealous lover is an oxymoron.

November 28: Jealousy is a spiritual wasteland. It stops up the soul with wanting and makes living in the present impossible.

November 29: "There is never jealousy where there is not strong regard," Washington Irving wrote. Take heart from all your jealous friends. They are the mark of your worth. Ignore them; they are their own worst enemies and they will self-destruct somewhere along the way.

November 30: Success is what I do to the best of my ability and with great joy, regardless of who else is doing it or how well.

DECEMBER

PSALM 1

*They are like trees
planted beside
flowing waters.
They yield fruit
in due season;
their leaves are
ever green.*

*hristmas is a strange season. When you're a child,
it is a season of presents. When you're young, it's
a season of parties. When you get your own
home, it's a season of preparations. But when you get
older, Christmas changes color drastically. Suddenly, out
from behind the advertisements and big dinners, through
the haze of old carols and soft candles, past the dazzling
altars and sumptuous crib scenes, we begin to see what
Christmas is really all about. Christmas is about finding
life where we did not expect life to be.*

*Every year of life waxes and wanes. Every stage of
life comes and goes. Every facet of life is born and then
dies. Every good moment is doomed to become only a
memory. Every perfect period of living slips through our
fingers and disappears. Every hope dims and every possibility turns eventually to dry clay. Until Christmas
comes again. Then we are called at the deepest, most
subconscious, least cognizant level to begin to live again.*

*Christmas brings us all back to the crib of life to start
over: aware of what has gone before, conscious that nothing can last, but full of hope that this time, finally, we
can learn what it takes to live well, grow to full stature
of soul and spirit, get it right.*

*There is a child in each of us waiting to be born again.
It is to those looking for life that the figure of the Christ,*

134

a child, beckons. Christmas is not for children. It is for those who refuse to give up and grow old, for those to whom life comes newly and with purpose each and every day, for those who can let yesterday go so that life can be full of new possibility always, for those who are agitated with newness whatever their age. Life is for the living, for those in whom Christmas is a feast without finish, a celebration of the constancy of change, a call to begin once more the journey to human joy and holy meaning.

December 1: "Life," Kierkegaard wrote, "can only be understood backwards; but it must be lived forwards." Try to remember that there is purpose in everything that happens to you. There will be times in life when you can neither believe nor accept that but, as time goes by, if you begin to watch for it carefully and learn to cultivate each moment well, you will come to taste the fruit of it. Then you will be fully alive.

December 2: We strive so hard for perfection and fullness of life. Yet, every year the Christ appears to us again as a child. There may be a lesson in that.

December 3: Don't ever be afraid to begin life in new ways. In fact, what else is life about? Pity those who drive to work exactly the same way every day. They will never, ever see the flowers in the yards on the other side of town. Being efficient, but brain-dead, may be living but it is not life.

December 4: It's nice to give Christmas parties for people. It's even nicer to be relaxed enough to enjoy them ourselves. Remember, the purpose of the gathering is gathering, not the work of doing it.

December 5: "The true meaning of life is to plant trees, under whose shade you do not expect to sit," Nelson Henderson wrote. It is what we leave behind to benefit the rest of the world that gives our own life value. What are you working on now that will make the world a gentler place for the children of tomorrow?

December 6: It is so easy to go through life without ever living it.

December 7: Everybody's life is unbalanced in one way or another. The perfect life is not the absolute arithmetical division of time between its segments of play, work, prayer, solitude, and family. The perfect life is the one in which we have grown into all these factors — ignoring none of them, celebrating all of them, cultivating each of them.

December 8: Every stage of life has something to teach us that enables us to live the next one with hope and courage. Think of the stages of your own life. What did you learn in each of them that is now part of your energy, your strength, and without which this one would not be possible?

December 9: Life never satisfies. It always draws us inexorably on, like a magnet, to life that is even greater. It is only the definition of greatness that is in question.

December 10: Some young people are very old both in their attitudes and in their worn-out, jaded, and satiated feelings. Some older people are very young. They stay devoted to learning new things and collecting new experiences. They discuss new ideas and go to new places. They love new loves and begin to live in new ways. "They are," as the psalmist says, "like trees... their leaves are ever green." They are a model to us all. They teach us that it isn't life that fails us; it is we who fail life.

December 11: Life, psychologists tell us, goes in cycles. Extroverts in one phase of it, we become introverts in a later phase of it. Business types at one age, we find ourselves intent on nature at another. We don't stay at one thing all our lives anymore; we live many different things at many different times. Clinging to the past, no matter how good it was, is not living; it is existence gone awry, the commitment of a butterfly to remain a caterpillar.

December 12: What the crib confronts us with every Christmas is the challenge to go into new things open, vulnerable, willing, and trusting. In the end, those may be the very qualities that separate the happy from the unhappy when life is finally over.

December 13: When we hand our lives over to other people — spouses, friends, authority figures — we reserve the right to blame everybody else for our discomforts. Better to risk losing every person whose disapproval I fear than to spend life resenting them for making it impossible for me to make my own mistakes.

December 14: Life is a series of closed doors which, if opened, lead us to new understandings of ourselves and which, if not, seal us off from the rest of ourselves to the point that we live half-lives forever.

December 15: Life is not a supermarket. Its real value lies in selecting experiences well, not in sampling all of them to the point that our senses are too glutted and dulled to tell one thing from another. Life deserves a taste so acute that we appreciate its small and subtle pieces as well as its great and glamorous ones.

December 16: Life lies in learning to listen to soft music in the still of night rather than concentrating on the fitfulness that comes when we have irritated our souls to the breaking point.

December 17: The Chinese say, "It is only when the cold season comes that we know the pine and cypress to be evergreens." The essence of life shines best when all the tinsel has been stripped away. When the children are grown and the work is slowing and accumulation has lost its glow and the pain of loss has set in, the little things begin to count. Hot coffee in the morning, flowers on the walk, a good book by the bedside, small boats and small streams become the treasures of life. Then, finally, we have learned to live.

December 18: Life has its seasons, we know: springtimes of newness, summers of accomplishment, autumns of appreciation, and winters of transition. What is most important to realize, perhaps, is that every segment of life goes through every season too. Whatever I am doing now, whatever I have done before, has all gone through every part of the cycle. It is the law of human growth and spiritual awakening.

December 19: What is so hard to understand is why we spend so much of life resisting it. We fight the changes, the moves, the shifts, the demands and then wonder why we are too worn out to enjoy it.

December 20: Everyone wrestles with something in life: the compliant with overextension, the rigid with encroachment, the just with pain, the idealistic with reality, the private types with public expectations, the social ones with solitude. Why? Because the compliant cannot really live until they learn to draw boundaries, the rigid until they loosen up, the just until they bring compassion to righteousness; the idealistic until they learn to deal with the mundane; the introverts until they begin to speak up and the extroverts until they begin to listen. Life is one long exercise in learning to experiment with new ways of being alive. Those who refuse will simply end up sitting on the side of the road while life goes by.

December 21: It isn't change that destroys life. It is when we make our lives a monument to old ideas and old ways of doing things — then life withers in mid-air.

December 22: We have nothing to do with our births and little to do with our deaths. It is only what separates the two that we have any control over at all. We can live it or we can simply wait for it to go by.

December 23: The scandal of the universe is that so many of us have the luxury to discuss the nature of life when so many of us can barely exist at all.

December 24: "Holy One," the disciples said. "Tell us the answer to the greatest spiritual question of them all: "Is there life after death?" And the Holy One replied, "The greatest spiritual question of them all is not, 'Is there life after death?' The greatest spiritual question of them all is, 'Is there life before death?'"

December 25: The function of the Christmas crib to those who view it carefully is to remind us that there is nothing in life that cannot come to fullness of life in us if we will only allow it.

December 26: The last time you took it upon yourself to begin something new in life was the last time you took life into your own hands.

December 27: The nice thing about running out of time is that we begin to use it differently. Old age may well be the one gift given us that enables us to get the best out of life.

December 28: All creation teaches us that life is one new beginning after another, one tree downed and one tree seeded after another, one flower picked and one flower planted after another. It is having the courage to end what is finished, to begin what is fragile that is the measure of life well lived.

December 29: When we stop planning bold, bright things for tomorrow, we have ended life long before it was meant to stop being new for us. Beware of those who stop living before your very eyes. They will poison your life as well as their own.

December 30: Jesus came in a crib so that we would all feel responsible for bringing goodness to life, for nurturing the impossible, for believing in the fragile things that make life worth living for everyone.

December 31: "If the only prayer you say in your life is 'thank you,'" Meister Eckhart wrote, "that would suffice." And after all, what else is there to say but thank you? Thank you for the people now dead who brought me to fullness of life; thank you for the experiences now gone that brought me to wholeness; thank you for the bliss that carried me through the burdensome parts of life ever hopeful of the next one.

ALSO BY

JOAN CHITTISTER

THE PSALMS
Meditations for Every Day of the Year

"Chittister's Christianity is alive with spiritual radiance that
makes the ordinary gleam with light and meaning."
— *Values & Vision*

0-8245-1581-1; $12.95

THE RULE OF BENEDICT
Insights for the Ages

Fresh insights from proven principles that chart the life of
many religious communities and that anyone wishing to live
a spiritual life will find useful.

0-8245-2503-5; $11.95

*At your bookstore or, to order directly from the publisher, please send
check or money order (including $3.00 shipping for the first book
and $1.00 for each additional book) to:*

THE CROSSROAD PUBLISHING COMPANY
370 LEXINGTON AVENUE, NEW YORK, NY 10017

We hope you enjoyed Songs of Joy. *Thank you for reading it.*

crossroad